Java Interview Guide

How to Build Confidence With a Solid Understanding of Core Java Principles

Anthony DePalma

Java Interview Guide
How to Build Confidence With a Solid Understanding of Core Java Principles

ISBN-13: 978-0692573426
ISBN-10: 0692573429

Editors: Ayesha Khan; Jonathan Hall
Design/Typesetting (Interior): Chris Moore www.fromprinttoebook.com

Table of Contents

Introduction

The Purpose of this Guide

This guide will prepare you for an interview to an entry-level or a senior-level position as a Java software developer. It's intended to be a high-level resource and it's assumed that you are already familiar with the Java language and know how to write basic applications.

The book is divided into chapters of related concepts that are presented in interview-sized chunks. At the end of each chapter is a series of potential interview questions. Read through each chapter and research any topics that are unfamiliar until you are able to answer every question confidently. All of the questions are listed again at the end of the book.

In order to get the most out of this guide, make sure that you are able to answer every question in your own words. From the perspective of an interviewer, it's always better to hear a candidate explain something uniquely, because it proves that you understand the underlying concepts. It will also prepare you for variations of the same questions. The stronger you understand the concepts, the more confident you'll appear in your interview. Are you ready?

The Java Programming Language

The History of Java

Java is an object-oriented programming language that was released
by Sun Microsystems in 1995. Unlike C++, it allowed developers
to write code that could run on multiple platforms. This principle,
called Write Once, Run Anywhere (WORA), prevented the need
for developers to write different applications for different operating
systems. Java borrowed much of its syntax from C++, but it streamlined
development by providing features such as automatic memory
management and by eliminating pitfalls such as multiple inheritance.

The Java Virtual Machine

The WORA principle is possible because of the Java Virtual Machine
(JVM). A virtual machine is software that emulates a physical machine.
In traditional programming languages, code is compiled into machine
language for a specific platform. In Java, code is compiled into a virtual
machine language called bytecode. The JVM acts as an intermediary
between bytecode and the underlying physical machine.

Every platform that supports Java has its own implementation of the JVM.
Java applications are portable because every JVM adheres to a standard
interface. The distribution package of the JVM and standard libraries
is called the Java Runtime Environment (JRE). The distribution package
of the JRE and development tools, such as the compiler and debugger,
is called the Java Development Kit (JDK).

THE JAVA PROGRAMMING LANGUAGE

Procedural Programming vs Object-Oriented Programming

Procedural programming is a style of writing code that executes a series
of linear procedures to produce a result. Object-oriented programming
is a style of writing code that uses objects to encapsulate state and behavior.
Procedural code is easier to use in small projects or in multithreaded
environments due to its stateless nature, but object-oriented code
is far more flexible and easier to maintain.

Questions

What is the WORA principle? Why is it beneficial?

How can Java applications run on multiple platforms?

What is the difference between the JRE and the JDK?

What is the difference between procedural programming
and object-oriented programming?

Object-Oriented Concepts

Abstraction

Abstraction is the act of perceiving an entity from a narrow perspective. For example, in the context of education a person can be reduced to a student, and in the context of employment a person can be reduced to an employee. Each abstraction reduces the attributes of a person to a subset of relevant information. The goal of abstraction is to reduce complexity in software systems.

Encapsulation

Encapsulation is a technique that encourages abstraction by purposefully hiding information. For example, the mechanical details of a car engine are encapsulated behind a steering wheel and floor pedals. Anyone familiar with this interface could drive a car without knowing what type of engine was under the hood. Java encourages encapsulation through the use of interfaces and by providing access modifiers that limit the visibility of classes, fields, and methods.

Polymorphism

Polymorphism is a technique that encourages abstraction by allowing an entity to assume multiple forms. For example, a smartphone is polymorphic because it can assume the role of a camera, web browser, music player, or digital clock. Each application exposes a relevant interface to the user. In Java, an object can take on the form of any parent in its hierarchy or any interface in its hierarchy.

Mutability

Mutability refers to the ability of an entity to change its state. An iPod is an example of a mutable entity because its contents frequently change. A vinyl record is an example of an immutable entity because its contents are permanently engraved. Immutable objects provide numerous benefits in software applications, such as stability and thread safety. `Strings` and all of the primitive wrapper objects are examples of immutable objects. In order to make an object immutable, the class must be `final`, all fields must be `final`, and it cannot expose any mutable fields or methods that modify mutable fields.

Coupling

Coupling refers to the level of dependency that exists between two entities. For example, a cell phone battery that is soldered to a motherboard is tightly coupled because neither the battery nor the motherboard can be replaced without affecting the other component. A battery that snaps into the back of a phone is loosely coupled because both entities could be replaced independently. In software applications, decoupled components are more flexible and easier to maintain.

Cohesion

Cohesion refers to an entity's level of focus. For example, a Swiss Army knife is a low cohesion entity because it can do multiple things, but it can't do them very well. A multi-tool could never match the productivity of a toolbox filled with highly cohesive tools. In software applications, cohesive components are more robust and easier to test.

Questions

What is the purpose of abstraction in software development?

What is encapsulation? How does Java support it?

What is polymorphism? How does Java support it?

What is the difference between a mutable object and an immutable object?

How can you design an object to be immutable?

What is the difference between coupling and cohesion?

What is the preferred relationship between software components and why?

Object-Oriented Programming (Part I)

Classes & Objects

Java objects are built from a blueprint called a class. A class defines the name of an object, what type of state the object has in the form of fields, and what kind of behavior the object has in the form of methods.

When an object is instantiated with the new keyword, the class file and all of its superclasses are loaded into the JVM by the system class loader. After the one-time initialization of the class, the object is initialized by invoking a special method called a constructor. A constructor performs initialization logic after recursively invoking all of the constructors of its superclasses. Superclasses must be initialized before subclasses in case a child object relies on functionality from a parent.

Primitive Types

A primitive type is a fixed-size data type that is predefined and reserved as a keyword. Primitive types serve as the building blocks for storing state in an object. There are eight primitive types: boolean, byte, short, int, long, float, double, and char. Primitive types are not objects, but every primitive type has a corresponding wrapper object.

The compiler can automatically convert primitive types into their wrapper objects in a process called autoboxing. Conversely, the compiler can convert wrapper objects into their primitive types in a process called unboxing. One common pitfall from unboxing occurs when a null object reference is unboxed into a primitive type, resulting in a NullPointerException.

Arrays

An array is an object that can hold a fixed number of values of a single type. The capacity of an array is defined when the array is initialized, and its elements can be accessed by a zero-based index. Arrays are covariant, meaning that an array can be cast to an array of its superclass type. For example, a `String[ ]` could be cast to an `Object[ ]`, because the `String` class extends the `Object` class.

Strings

Strings are unique objects that are used to represent text. String values can be assigned without the use of the `new` keyword, although the compiler is actually creating `String` objects internally. Strings can be concatenated via the overloaded + operator, which the compiler converts into a chain of method calls on a `StringBuilder` object. A `StringBuilder` (and thread-safe alternative `StringBuffer`) improves performance by modifying a mutable `char[ ]` buffer before creating an immutable `String` instance. The immutable property of strings allows the compiler to cache them in a process called interning.

Enums

Enums, short for enumerated types, are special classes that represent a set of single-instance constants. Practical applications include the days of the week, the status levels of a task, or the roles of a security group. Enums were introduced to replace `String` and `Integer` constants and they are far more powerful because they can contain methods, implement interfaces, and provide type safety. However, enums cannot be subclassed or extend any class besides the implicitly extended `Enum` class.

Packages

Classes and other resources are organized into folders with unique namespaces called packages. Packages are commonly organized by two competing methodologies: *package-by-layer* and *package-by-feature*.

A *package-by-layer* strategy groups classes together according to their layer in an application. For example, a *package-by-layer* structure might include a model, controller, service, dao, and utility package. *Package-by-layer* works for small applications, but it doesn't scale well due to the large number of tightly coupled classes that span a relatively small number of packages.

A *package-by-feature* strategy groups classes together according to their cohesiveness in an application. For example, a *package-by-feature* structure might include a customer, order, product, review, and report package. *Package-by-feature* encourages high modularity and loose coupling and is preferable to *package-by-layer*.

Questions

What is the difference between a class and an object?

What happens when an object is instantiated for the first time?

What is the difference between a primitive type and an object?

What is the difference between autoboxing and unboxing?

What is an array?

How is a String different from a regular object?

What is the difference between a StringBuilder and a StringBuffer?

Why are enums superior to String or Integer constants?

What is the difference between package-by-layer and package-by-feature?

Object-Oriented Programming (Part II)

Methods

Methods contain the logic that provide an object with behavior. A method declaration contains a list of modifiers, a return type, a method name, a list of parameter types and their corresponding names, and a list of throwable exceptions. A method signature is the combination of the method name as well as the types and order of its parameters. Note that the names of parameters are not included in the method signature.

A method can invoke itself in a process called recursion. Recursion is an alternative to looping that provides an elegant solution for problems that naturally repeat, such as mathematical sequences or divide and conquer algorithms. A recursive method must have a termination condition that determines when the method stops calling itself and starts returning values to previous invocations on the call stack. A recursive method with no termination condition will eventually cause a `StackOverflowError`.

Pass-by-Reference vs Pass-by-Value

The manner in which arguments are passed to methods depends on whether a programming language is *pass-by-reference* or *pass-by-value*. For example, imagine flying a kite and passing control of the kite to a friend. *Pass-by-reference* would be akin to handing the string over to them, but *pass-by-value* would require tying a duplicate string to the same kite and passing that instead. In both scenarios your friend could exert control over the kite, but with *pass-by-reference* your friend has the freedom to change what kite the string points to (or to let it go completely).

Every argument in Java is *pass-by-value*. With a primitive argument, the value of the primitive is copied and passed to the method. With an object argument, a pointer to the object is copied and passed to the method.

The Final Keyword

The `final` keyword determines whether an object reference can be changed after being assigned. In the kite example, using the `final` keyword would be akin to supergluing the string to your hand. The `final` keyword is often used in conjunction with the `static` keyword to create constants. However, it's important to note that the `final` keyword does not prevent an object's internal state from changing. The `final` keyword can also be applied at the class level to prevent subclasses from extending a class, or at the method level to prevent subclasses from overriding a method.

The Static Keyword

The `static` keyword determines whether a property belongs to a class or to an object instance. For example, imagine holding a blueprint for a house. Properties that can be unique between houses, such as the number of windows or doors, are examples of instance properties. Properties that can be written on the blueprint, such as the number of houses built, are examples of static properties. An object can access static properties on a class, but a class cannot access instance properties unless it holds a reference to an object.

Access Modifiers

Access modifiers determine the visibility of classes, fields, and methods, so that information can be hidden in order to reduce complexity. The four types of access modifiers are:

`Public` – Visible to all classes.
`Protected` – Visible to subclasses and classes in the same package.
`<None>` – Visible to classes in the same package.
`Private` – Visible to the enclosing class.

Annotations

Annotations can be applied to fields, methods, classes, and packages to embed metadata alongside code. Annotations alone have no effect on a codebase, but they can be detected during compile-time or during runtime to provide additional functionality. For example, the `@Override` annotation can be used on methods that override a superclass method, allowing the compiler to prevent bugs due to invalid method signatures. The `@Column(name)` annotation can be used to map fields to database columns, allowing data access objects to dynamically generate SQL queries at runtime.

Questions

What is the difference between a method declaration and a method signature?

What is a recursive method?

What is the final keyword used for?

What is the static keyword used for?

Why can't a static method access a nonstatic field?

What are access modifiers used for? What are the different types?

What are annotations used for?

The Object Superclass

Every class in Java is a descendent, directly or indirectly, of the `Object` class. The `Object` class provides several methods that can be optionally extended in subclasses.

Clone

The `clone()` method was originally designed to return a copy of an object that implements the `Cloneable` interface. A clone can either be a shallow copy, which shares the same references as the original object, or a deep copy, which copies the values of the original object into new objects. Unfortunately, overriding this method correctly is difficult and it provides no benefit over a copy constructor, which offers more flexibility and a cleaner contract.

Equals

The `equals()` method compares two objects for equality. The default implementation relies on the identity operator (`==`) to determine whether two objects point to the same address in memory. Subclasses are encouraged to override this method to test whether two objects contain the same information rather than the same location in memory. Note that if you override the `equals()` method you must by contract override the `hashCode()` method as well.

HashCode

The `hashCode()` method digests the state of an object into an integer, which is primarily useful for hash table data structures. By default, the hash code is implemented by converting the internal address of an object into an integer. The hash code must be consistently returned and should always

return equal values for objects that are equal according to the
`equals()` method.

ToString

The `toString()` method returns a textual representation of an
object, which is primarily useful for logging and debugging. By default,
the `toString()` method returns the class of the object followed
by a hexadecimal representation of its hash code value.

GetClass

The `getClass()` method returns a `Class` object that contains
information about a class and utility methods for reflection-based access
to fields and methods. The `getClass()` method is final and cannot
be overridden by subclasses.

Finalize

The `finalize()` method was originally designed to be invoked before
an object was destroyed by the garbage collector. However, an object
might not become eligible for garbage collection if it's never dereferenced
or if the application exits before the garbage collector runs. It's generally
discouraged to rely on this method for cleanup operations due to its
uncertainty and the possibility that an object can be unintentionally
revived by creating additional references to it.

Wait, Notify, NotifyAll

The final methods `wait()`, `notify()`, and `notifyAll()` provide
low-level concurrency operations that allow communication between
threads. For example, one thread could halt its execution until it receives
a notification from another thread. Java provides high-level concurrent
data structures in the `java.util.concurrent` package.

Questions

What is the difference between a shallow copy and a deep copy?

Why is a copy constructor preferable to the clone method?

What is the difference between the identity operator and the equals() method?

What is the relationship between the hashCode() method and the equals() method?

What is the default implementation of the toString() method?

Why is the finalize() method unreliable for cleanup operations?

Composition & Inheritance

Composition   HAS A

Composition is a technique that prevents code duplication by delegating functionality to other objects. For example, a `Party` class could delegate method calls to a `List` object to provide functionality for a guest list. This would allow the `Party` class to selectively expose methods such as `addGuest()` instead of exposing every method in the `List` interface.

Inheritance   IS A

Inheritance is a technique that prevents code duplication by inheriting functionality from parent objects. For example, a `Party` class could extend an `ArrayList` to provide functionality for a guest list. This would allow `Party` objects to be used in enhanced for-loops or methods that accept a `List`. Multiple inheritance is not allowed in order to prevent the ambiguity that arises when multiple parents implement the same feature independently. This ambiguity is called *The Diamond Problem* (or *The Deadly Diamond of Death*) due to the shape of the resulting object hierarchy.

Method Overriding vs Method Overloading

Method overriding allows a subclass to change the functionality of a superclass. This occurs when a subclass defines a non-static method with the same method signature as a parent method. As of Java 5, the overridden method can declare either the same return type or a covariant (subclassed) return type. An overridden method will be invoked even when an object is cast to its parent's type.

Method overriding is commonly confused with method overloading. Method overloading occurs when two or more methods in a class have the same name with different method signatures. Method overloading provides an API with flexibility by allowing clients to call up an appropriate version of a method without having to pass in `null` values for optional parameters.

Composition vs Inheritance

Composition and inheritance both provide code reuse, but it can be difficult to determine which relationship is more appropriate. As a general rule, ask whether two objects share a *HAS-A* or an *IS-A* relationship. For example, a party *HAS-A* guest list, so it follows that a `Party` should be composed of a `List`. On the other hand, a student *IS-A* person, so it follows that a `Student` should inherit from a `Person`.

Although both methods are powerful, they each have their own weaknesses. Composition requires delegation code and prevents polymorphism unless additional interfaces are introduced. Inheritance forces a rigid object hierarchy and tightly couples two classes. When in doubt, composition is the preferred approach because it's more flexible than inheritance.

Questions

What is the difference between composition and inheritance?

What is the difference between method overriding and method overloading?

How would you determine whether to use composition or inheritance?

Abstract Classes & Interfaces

Abstract Classes

Abstract classes are designed to be extended and cannot be instantiated. For example, an abstract class `Person` might contain common attributes and rely on concrete subclasses like `Employee` and `Student` to provide additional functionality. An abstract class can have both concrete and abstract methods, but it can only be instantiated by a concrete subclass that implements every abstract method somewhere along the object hierarchy.

Interfaces

Interfaces promote polymorphism by describing a form that an object can take. For example, imagine a government agency that is interested in taxing people. Rather than tightly couple their codebase to the `Student` and `Employee` objects, they could instead introduce a `Taxable` interface and require people to provide their own implementations. Interfaces can only contain constant fields and empty methods. A class can implement more than one interface, but it must provide the implementation for every method (duplicate methods are treated as one).

Abstract Classes vs Interfaces

It's a common misconception to assume that abstract classes and interfaces compete for functionality; in practice they frequently work together. For example, Java's `AbstractList` class partially implements methods from the `List` interface, lessening the burden for subclasses such as `ArrayList` and `LinkedList`. In general, abstract classes are used to plan an inheritance hierarchy and simplify the work of subclasses. Interfaces are used to introduce a layer of abstraction and decouple modules of code.

Anonymous Classes

In order to reduce the verbosity of the language, Java allows anonymous classes to be instantiated with the new keyword. For example, every button in a Swing application has an ActionListener that is invoked when the button is clicked. Rather than create a new class file for every action, you could instead declare anonymous classes that implement the ActionListener interface.

Anonymous classes provide support for closures. A closure is a block of code that can be passed around while maintaining access to variables of the enclosing scope. For example, a button that changes the title of a Swing application would need a closure to access the window frame. Although it may appear that anonymous classes have direct access to enclosing variables, in fact the variables are copied in the same manner as method arguments (*pass-by-value*). In order to prevent ambiguity, all enclosing variables must be declared final before they can be accessed by an anonymous class.

Java 8 provides even more succinct support for closures in the form of lambda expressions. A lambda expression is a single-line representation of an anonymous class that contains a single method.

Questions

What is the difference between an abstract class and an interface?

How would you determine whether to use an abstract class
or an interface?

Why can't a class be declared both final and abstract?

What is the value of designing a codebase around
the use of interfaces?

What are anonymous classes used for?

What is a closure?

What is a lambda expression?

Throwable Class
↓
Error

Exceptions

Runtime Exception
↓   ↓   unchecked
NullPointer   ClassCast   Exception
Exception   Exception   ↓

Illegal Argument
Exception

Exceptions are special objects that are thrown whenever an error interrupts the normal execution of code. All exceptions are descendents of the Throwable class and are divided into two categories: unchecked exceptions and checked exceptions.

Unchecked Exceptions

Unchecked exceptions represent a defect in the application, such as invoking a method on a null object reference or casting an object to an invalid type. A method can throw an unchecked exception without forcing its callers to establish an error-handling policy. Unchecked exceptions extend the RuntimeException class. Common unchecked exceptions include NullPointerExceptions, IllegalArgumentExceptions, and ClassCastExceptions.

Checked Exceptions

Checked exceptions represent a defect that occurs outside of the control of the application, such as opening a file that doesn't exist or connecting to a database with invalid credentials. A method that throws a checked exception forces its callers to establish an error-handling policy. Callers must either surround the method in a try/catch block or add the exception to its method declaration to push the responsibility further up the call stack. Checked exceptions extend the Exception class. Common checked exceptions include IOExceptions, FileNotFoundExceptions, and InterruptedExceptions.

checked Exception   (try/catch)

IO Exception
File Not Found Exception
Interrupted Exception   ((
                                          [31])

Unchecked Exceptions vs Checked Exceptions

Checked exceptions have been a source of contention in the Java community because they are frequently overused. The official documentation states: "*If a client can reasonably be expected to recover from an exception, make it a checked exception. If a client cannot do anything to recover from the exception, make it an unchecked exception.*" When in doubt, unchecked exceptions are preferred because it allows clients to choose whether or not an error-handling policy is appropriate.

Errors

An `Error` is thrown by the JVM to indicate that a fatal condition has occurred. Errors extend the `Throwable` class directly, which gives them the behavior of unchecked exceptions. Common errors include `OutOfMemoryErrors` or `StackOverflowErrors`.

Try/Catch/Finally

Java provides three keywords that are used to establish an error-handling policy. The `try` keyword delineates a block of code that might throw an exception. The `catch` keyword designates a handler for a specific type of exception. An exception that is thrown within a `try` block will be caught by the first `catch` block whose exception type either matches the thrown exception or is a superclass of the thrown exception.

The `finally` keyword delineates a block of code that will be invoked regardless of whether or not an exception was thrown. A `finally` block is generally used to provide cleanup operations. For example, code that attempts to update a database might be surrounded with a `finally` block because the database connection should be closed regardless of whether or not the update was successful.

Try-With-Resources

Java 7 introduced the *try-with-resources* statement, which allowed resources that implement the `AutoCloseable` interface to be declared as parameters inside of the `try` block. When the `try` block completes, the JVM will automatically call the `close()` method on those resources, eliminating the need for a `finally` block.

Questions

What is an exception?

What is the difference between an unchecked and a checked exception?

How would you determine whether to use an unchecked or a checked exception?

How does a try/catch/finally block work?

How does the try-with-resources statement work?

Generics

Compile-Time Errors vs Runtime Errors

Compile-time errors are errors that prevent a program from compiling, such as syntax errors. Runtime errors are errors that occur during the execution of an application, such as casting an object to an invalid type. Compile-time errors are easier to fix because the compiler tells you where they occur. Runtime errors are more difficult to detect and may cause unpredictable behavior in unrelated parts of the application. It is therefore preferable to catch as many errors as possible during the compile-time phase.

Generics

Generics were introduced to prevent runtime errors caused by invalid type casting. For example, it would be legal to add a `String` to a non-generic `List` and retrieve it with a cast to an `Integer`, resulting in a `ClassCastException`. However the same situation with a generic `List<String>` would cause a compile-time error. Without generics, the only way to accomplish type safety would require a `List` implementation for every possible object, such as a `StringList`, `IntegerList`, etc.

Generic Wildcards

Unlike arrays, generics are invariant, meaning that generic objects do not share the same relationship as its types. For example, even though `Integer` extends `Number`, `List<Integer>` does not extend `List<Number>`. The common parent of `List<Integer>` and `List<Number>` is the wildcard type `List<?>`.

Wildcards can be used to create restrictions on generic types. For example, the upper bounded wildcard `List<? extends Number>` allows the

Number type and all subclasses of Number. The lower bounded wildcard List<? super Number> allows the Number type and all superclasses of Number.

Type Erasure

In order to preserve backwards compatibility, generic types are removed by the compiler and replaced with object casts in a process called type erasure. Type erasure prevents the need for legacy code to be recompiled, but it also introduces several limitations. For example, generic exceptions are not allowed because a catch block cannot tell the difference between a GenericException<String> and a GenericException<Integer>. Similarly, a class cannot implement both Comparable<String> and Comparable<Integer>, because without generic types they both represent the same interface.

Questions

What is the difference between a compile-time error and a runtime error?

What is the purpose of generics?

What are the different types of generic wildcards?

What is type erasure?

What are some of the limitations of generics?

Concurrency

Java supports concurrent programming through the use of threads.
A thread is a single path of execution in an application. The JVM
typically launches as a single process, spawning multiple threads that
share its resources. Threads that modify shared resources must be
coordinated in order to prevent unpredictable behavior.

Thread Lifecycle

— runnable
—running
—dies

A thread is born by instantiating a subclass of the `Thread` class, or by
instantiating a `Thread` object with a `Runnable` argument. A thread
enters a runnable state when its `start()` method is invoked. The JVM
uses a priority-based scheduling algorithm to determine which thread
to execute. A thread enters a running state when its `run()` method is
invoked by the scheduler. However, a thread can transition into a blocked
state if it needs to acquire a lock or if it waits for a notification from
another thread. A thread dies after the `run()` method completes.

Synchronization

Synchronization is required on mutable resources because the operations
of multiple threads can interleave. For example, the `c++` operation may
appear to be atomic, but it is actually composed of three steps: read the
value of `c`, increment the value of `c`, and write the value of `c`. If one thread
reads the value of `c` and enters a blocked state, a second thread could read
the same value and the counter would only be incremented by one.
Synchronizing access to the `c++` operation would force all three steps
to be completed atomically.

Although synchronization can prevent thread interference and memory
consistency errors, it can also degrade performance and open up the

((

possibility of a deadlock. A deadlock occurs when two threads wait for each to proceed.

The Synchronize Keyword

The synchronize keyword is used to designate synchronized methods and statements. A synchronized block of code is guarded by a lock that can only be acquired by one thread at a time. In a synchronized static method, the singleton Class object is implicitly used as the lock. In a synchronized non-static method, the object instance is implicitly used as the lock. In a synchronized statement, the lock must be provided as an argument. Multiple locks allow for more granular levels of synchronization.

For example, imagine a Counter class with a synchronized count() method. If the count() method was static, only one thread in the application could increment the counter at a time. If the count() method was non-static, multiple Counter objects could be instantiated and incremented concurrently. If the Counter class had two separate variables and two separate count() methods, each method could use synchronized statements with different locks so that both variables could be incremented concurrently.

The Volatile Keyword

The volatile keyword is used to indicate that the value of a variable may be modified by multiple threads. Java's memory model permits threads to cache the value of variables for performance. The volatile keyword must be used if a method relies on the latest value of a shared variable. For example, a method that executes a while(!finished) loop would need to declare the finished variable as volatile if a separate thread was responsible for updating its value.

The guarantee that a memory write will be visible to another block of code is called a *happens-before* relationship. Both the volatile keyword and the synchronize keyword guarantee a *happens-before* relationship, however the `synchronize` keyword also guarantees atomic access to a block of code.

Concurrent Data Structures

Java 5 introduced several high-level data structures in the `java.util.concurrent` package. `CopyOnWriteArrayList` is a thread-safe alternative to `ArrayList` that copies the underlying array during modifications. `ConcurrentHashMap` is a thread-safe alternative to `HashMap` that only incurs a synchronization penalty on segments of the map that were modified. The `BlockingQueue` was introduced to allow producers to block and wait while a queue is full, and allow consumers to block and wait while a queue is empty.

The Executor Framework

The executor framework provides a layer of abstraction over multithreaded task execution. The `ExecutorService` manages a thread pool that accepts `Runnable` or `Callable` tasks. Submitting a task immediately returns a `Future` object, which contains methods that return the status and result of a running task. The executor framework effectively decouples tasks from their execution policies.

ThreadLocal Storage

The `ThreadLocal` class allows values to be stored inside of the currently running `Thread` object. For example, imagine tracing an HTTP request that starts in a servlet and traverses through a service. Rather than pass a transaction ID as an argument in every method, you could instead store the ID in a `ThreadLocal` object and retrieve it statically along the way. `ThreadLocal` variables reduce the verbosity of methods, but care must be taken to ensure that a value is removed if the thread is returned to a thread pool.

Atomic Variables

Wait free / lock free

Java introduced several variables with built-in concurrency such as `AtomicInteger`, `AtomicLong`, and `AtomicBoolean`. For example, an `AtomicInteger` could replace and even outperform our `Counter` class because it's implemented with native method calls. A native method call executes outside of the JVM in a platform-dependent programming language.

Questions

What is the lifecycle of a Thread?

Why is synchronization necessary on shared resources?

What is used as a lock for synchronized static and synchronized non-static methods?

What would happen if two different threads hit two synchronized non-static methods on the same object simultaneously?

What would happen if two different threads hit a synchronized static method and synchronized non-static method on the same object simultaneously?

What one thing does the volatile keyword guarantee about a variable?

What two things does the synchronize keyword guarantee about a block of code?

What are some built-in concurrent data structures?

What is the executor framework?

What is a ThreadLocal variable?

What are atomic variables?

Memory Management

Heap Memory

Java objects reside in a dynamically sized area of memory called the heap. The heap is divided into young generation objects and old generation objects. In a typical application, the vast majority of objects are short lived. In order to improve performance, surviving objects are migrated to the old generation heap space where they are ignored during the aggressive garbage collection of the young generation heap space.

Garbage Collection

The garbage collection routine is automatically invoked when the heap fills up. The garbage collector identifies objects that are no longer referenced by the application and removes them to free up memory. The garbage collector can be manually invoked through the `System.gc()` method, but there is no guarantee when the process will start.

The algorithm used for garbage collection is called mark and sweep. In the first step, objects that are referenced in memory are identified and marked. In the second step, unmarked objects are deleted, freeing up chunks of memory. The remaining memory can then be compacted into contiguous blocks in a process similar to defragmenting a hard drive.

Strong References

A strong reference is a typical reference such as assigning an object to a variable or putting an object in an array. A strong reference to an object guarantees that the object will remain on the heap. An object is eligible for garbage collection if it cannot be accessed through any chain of strong references.

Strong references can accumulate over time. When an application uses more memory than the allocated heap space, the result is an `OutOfMemoryError`. When an application fills up the heap with unintentional references, the result is a memory leak. `OutOfMemoryErrors` can be fixed by allocating a larger heap size through JVM arguments, but a memory leak could eventually fill up a heap of any size.

Memory Leaks

Memory leaks are possible despite Java's automatic memory management. For example, imagine hosting the world's largest star database. In order to improve performance we could use a `ConcurrentMap` to cache a `Star` object, using its name as a key. However, as more and more users looked up stars, our `Star` cache would grow like a black hole until it eventually consumed all of the available heap space. Fortunately, Java provides different `Reference` objects to prevent this problem.

Memory leaks are often difficult to locate, since the resulting `OutOfMemoryError` could be thrown from any part of the application. Debugging a memory leak usually requires the help of a profiler. A profiler can analyze the heap dump created when the JVM crashes and recreate the reference hierarchy to pinpoint where the majority of memory is being retained.

Soft References

A soft reference is an object that can only be retrieved by invoking the `get()` method on a `SoftReference` container. Softly reachable objects will not be eagerly garbage collected, making them ideal for caches. For example, if we stored `SoftReference<Star>` values inside of our map, our cache could grow until it filled the heap, at which point the `get()` method would start returning `null` for stars that were garbage collected. We could then treat these values as if they were expired cache entries.

Weak References

A weak reference is an object that can only be retrieved by invoking the get() method on a WeakReference container. Weakly reachable objects will be eagerly garbage collected, making them ideal for short-lived object associations. For example, if we allowed our users to edit stars, we could use a ConcurrentMap to synchronize access to a star by associating its name to a User. However, if the user closed their browser prematurely the star would remain locked in the map. Assuming that the User was also stored as a strong reference in a session object, we could use a WeakReference<User> to determine when that session expired because the get() method would return null soon after the session was garbage collected.

Reference Queue

In both of our examples, there is a subtle problem.
Our SoftReference<Star> cache automatically removes Star objects, but we could still fill up the map with keys and empty SoftReference containers. Fortunately, Java provides us with an elegant solution in the form of a ReferenceQueue.

A ReferenceQueue is a queue that can be passed into the constructor of Reference objects. When an object wrapped by a Reference becomes garbage collected, the Reference is enqueued onto the ReferenceQueue. This queue can then be polled for cleanup operations. If we were to subclass the SoftReference and WeakReference classes to store the name of a star, we would then have a convenient callback for removing expired map entries.

Phantom References

A phantom reference is an object that is wrapped inside of
a `PhantomReference` container. However, invoking the `get()`
method on a `PhantomReference` will always return `null`. A phantom
reference in conjunction with a reference queue provides a safer alternative
to the `finalize()` method because there is no possibility of reviving
a dead object with new references.

Questions

How does the JVM divide memory on the heap?

What is the standard algorithm for garbage collection?

What are memory leaks? How can they be identified?

What are the four different types of references?

What is a ReferenceQueue?

Why is a phantom reference safer than using the finalize()
method?

Java Database Connectivity

The Java Database Connectivity (JDBC) API is an interface for querying and updating a database.

Connection

The Connection interface encapsulates the communication to a database. A Connection is provided by either a DriverManager or a DataSource. A DriverManager requires connection details such as the url and credentials, but a DataSource hides the connection details behind an interface. A DataSource is usually provided by an application server through a lookup service called the Java Naming and Directory Interface (JNDI). DataSources are preferable to DriverManagers because they are more flexible and easier to change.

Statements

Statements are provided by a Connection to encapsulate SQL queries. PreparedStatements are pre-compiled by the database and improve performance for queries that are executed repeatedly or contain input parameters. CallableStatements are used to execute stored procedures that contain both input and output parameters.

ResultSets

ResultSets are provided by Statements to encapsulate the result of a query. A ResultSet contains a cursor that can scroll through rows and extract type-safe values. ResultSets can be configured to support bidirectional scrolling as well as row modifications depending on the capabilities of the database.

SQL Injection

SQL injection is a popular attack vector that allows malicious queries to be embedded into `Statements` that were constructed out of string concatenations. SQL injection can be prevented by using `PreparedStatements` to register input values.

Object-Relational Mapping

Object-relational mapping (ORM) is a technique that bridges the gap between objects and relational databases. An ORM decouples the persistence layer of an application by generating SQL queries automatically. However, the relationship between objects and tables needs to be defined through configuration files, and it can be difficult to map complicated object hierarchies or address performance concerns for queries that are automatically generated. Hibernate is a popular ORM tool that is often used in conjunction with the Spring framework.

Questions

What is JDBC?

What are the two ways of acquiring a Connection object?

What is the difference between the three types of Statements?

What is a ResultSet?

What is an SQL injection attack? How can it be prevented?

What are the advantages and disadvantages
of object-relational mapping?

What is Hibernate?

Web Applications

A web application is software that is delivered by a server and rendered
by a browser. Java provides support for web applications through the
Servlet API.

The Servlet API

The Servlet API provides the specification for a servlet container.
A servlet container handles an HTTP request by delegating the request
to a web application, which in turn delegates the request to a `Servlet`.

A web application is packed into a web archive called a WAR file. A WAR
file contains classes, libraries, and a deployment descriptor called *web.xml*.
A deployment descriptor is a configuration file that describes how an
application should be deployed. For example, the *web.xml* file tells the
servlet container which URL patterns map to `Servlets`.

Servlets

`Servlets` are singleton objects that are managed by a servlet container.
The container invokes the `init()` method when the servlet is initially
loaded. Incoming requests are delegated to the `service()` method
concurrently. Finally, the container invokes the `destroy()` method
when the application is shutting down.

`HttpServlet` is a `Servlet` implementation that contains
methods corresponding to HTTP requests, such as `doGet()`,
`doPost()`, `doPut()`, and `doDelete()`. `HttpServlet` provides
access to request parameters as well as a session object that can store state
across requests. Sessions are correlated by an identifier that is stored in
a cookie by the browser.

JavaServer Pages

`Servlets` are notoriously clumsy at constructing HTML documents through Java code. JavaServer Pages (JSP) are text documents that contain static and dynamic content through the use of tags and a unified expression language (EL). JSPs are compiled into `Servlets` and have implicit access to the request and response objects.

`Servlets` and JSPs frequently work together through a `RequestDispatcher`. A `RequestDispatcher` transfers control of a request from one resource to another. For example, a servlet typically handles the logic for a request and delegates to a JSP to render the response.

Filters

`Filters` intercept servlet requests to provide cross-cutting functionality. For example, a security filter could redirect unauthenticated users to a login page. Filters are mapped to URL patterns in the deployment descriptor.

Model-View-Controller

Model-view-controller (MVC) is a design pattern that encourages the separation of concerns in a web application. The model represents domain objects, such as data retrieved from a database. The view is a visualization of the model, such as a JSP that constructs an HTML document. The controller facilitates changes to the model, such as a `Servlet` that handles the submission of a form. Multiple frameworks exist to facilitate the MVC pattern, such as Spring MVC.

Questions

What is a servlet container?

What is a web application?

What is a WAR file?

What is a web.xml file?

What is the difference between a Servlet and an HttpServlet?

What is the difference between a Servlet and a JSP?

What is a servlet filter?

What is the model-view-controller pattern?

Web Services

Service-Oriented Architecture

Service-oriented architecture (SOA) is a pattern that provides services to clients over a network. Services span a wide array of applications, including anything from delivering emails to generating random numbers via atmospheric noise.

Web Services

A web service is an implementation of SOA over the internet. Web services expose a contract that is independent of platforms or programming languages. The two most popular implementations are Simple Object Access Protocol (SOAP) and Representational State Transfer (REST).

SOAP

SOAP is a communication protocol that uses XML to define a Web Services Description Language (WSDL). The API described by WSDL documents can be parsed by consumers to generate classes automatically. The Java API for XML Web Services (JAX-WS) provides the specification for producing SOAP-based web services via annotations. Apache CXF is a popular open source implementation of JAX-WS.

REST

REST is a pattern for designing web services that rely on the HTTP protocol alone. REST web services expose meaningful URLs that utilize the GET, POST, PUT, and DELETE methods to access resources. REST architecture does not specify a standard data format, but JSON is frequently used as a lightweight alternative to XML. The Java API for RESTful Web Services (JAX-RS) provides the specification for producing REST-based web services via annotations. Jersey is a popular open source implementation of JAX-RS.

SOAP vs REST

SOAP web services are useful when a rigid contract is required to support complex operations between tightly coupled systems. REST web services are more flexible, but the lack of a WSDL document can be prohibitive for complex services. SOAP web services are generally slower than REST due to the verbosity of XML payloads.

Questions

What is service-oriented architecture?

What are web services?

What is the difference between a SOAP web service and a REST web service?

What is the difference between JAX-WS and JAX-RS?

What are some frameworks that aid in the development of Java web services?

Algorithms

Big O Notation

Big O notation measures the complexity of an operation relative to the size of its input.

`O(1)` describes an algorithm whose complexity is independent of the input, such as accessing an element in an array by its index.

`O(n)` describes an algorithm whose complexity increases linearly, such as iterating through an array.

`O(n^2)` describes an algorithm whose complexity increases quadratically, such as comparing every element in an array to every other element in an array.

`O(log n)` describes an algorithm whose complexity increases logarithmically, such as dividing an array in half until only one element remains.

`O(n log n)` describes an algorithm whose complexity increases linearithmically, such as dividing an array in half and iterating through each half.

Binary Search

Binary search is an `O(log n)` algorithm that is used to find a value in a sorted list of items. It works by searching for a value in the middle of a list, and recursively discarding whichever half of the list is out of range. The result of a binary search is undetermined if the list is unsorted. Binary search is available in the `Arrays` and `Collections` classes.

Insertion Sort

Insertion sort is an `O(n^2)` average-case sorting algorithm. It works by traversing through a list and sorting the previous elements by swapping them in place. Insertion sort is a stable algorithm, which means equal values will maintain their relative order. Insertion sort performs well for small data sets despite its complexity because it's efficient for partially sorted lists and it requires no extra memory.

Merge Sort

Merge sort is a stable `O(n log n)` average-case sorting algorithm. It works by recursively dividing a list into individual sublists, and merging each sublist together to produce a sorted result. Merge sort is an example of a divide and conquer algorithm, which recursively reduces a problem to a trivial solution.

Quicksort

Quicksort is an unstable `O(n log n)` average-case sorting algorithm. It works by defining a pivot and swapping elements so that lesser values appear before the pivot and greater values appear after the pivot. The remaining pivots are sorted recursively. As of Java 7, quicksort is the default implementation for sorting primitives in the `Arrays` class.

Timsort

Timsort is a stable `O(n log n)` average-case sorting algorithm. Timsort is a hybrid algorithm derived from merge sort and insertion sort. It works by identifying runs of naturally sorted data or by using insertion sort to create runs of a minimum size. The runs are merged together in the same manner as merge sort. Timsort often performs far fewer than `O(n log n)` comparisons because it takes advantage of partially sorted values. As of Java 7, Timsort is the default implementation for sorting objects in the `Arrays` and `Collections` classes.

Questions

What is Big O notation? What are some common examples?

What is a binary search? How well does it perform?

What is insertion sort? How well does it perform?

What is merge sort? How well does it perform?

What is quicksort? How well does it perform?

What is timsort? How well does it perform?

Java Collections Framework

The Java Collections Framework (JCF) provides common data structures that implement the `Collection` interface. A collection is an abstract representation of a generic group of objects.

List

(handwritten annotation: ArrayList ← LinkedList, CopyOnWriteArrayList)

A `List` is a data structure that holds an indexed collection. The `ArrayList` class uses an object array to hold its values. The values are copied into a larger array if the capacity is exceeded, but this can be avoided by specifying an initial capacity in the constructor. `ArrayList` is not thread-safe, but `CopyOnWriteArrayList` is a thread-safe alternative.

The `LinkedList` class uses a chain of `Node` objects to create a dynamically-sized list. A node contains a value along with a reference to the previous node and the next node in the chain. This allows nodes to be inserted or removed without reorganizing the list, but it requires iterating through the list to access an element by its index. `LinkedList` is not thread-safe, but it can be decorated by the `Collections#synchronizedList()` method.

Map

A `Map` is a data structure that associates keys with values. The `HashMap` class uses an array of linked lists to store `Entry` objects. An entry contains a key, a value, and a reference to the next entry in the chain. When you put a key/value pair in the map, a mathematical function such as the modulo operator (`%`) constrains the key's hash code to an index in the array. Unique keys that map to the same index are linked together, but duplicate keys will overwrite the existing entries. When you look up a value by key, the index is computed again and every entry in the linked list is inspected until a matching key is found.

HashMap requires that keys implement the hashCode() and equals() methods correctly. If the hash code is not unique, performance of the map will suffer because the linked lists will grow disproportionately. If the hash code is not consistent, entries can get lost in the map and leak memory.

If the size of a HashMap exceeds 75% of its capacity, the array is doubled and all of the entries are rehashed. This can be avoided by specifying an initial capacity and its load factor in the constructor. HashMap does not maintain the insertion order of its entries, but LinkedHashMap provides that functionality by storing its entries in an auxiliary LinkedList. HashMap is not thread-safe, but ConcurrentHashMap is a thread-safe alternative.

Deque

Stack → double ended – LIFO
Queue → FIFO
double ended

A Deque (double-ended queue) is a data structure that can insert or retrieve values from two sides. A deque that removes elements in a *last-in-first-out* (LIFO) policy is called a stack. A deque that removes elements in a *first-in-first-out* (FIFO) policy is called a queue. The ArrayDeque class uses an object array to store its values. ArrayDeque can be used as a stack or a queue, and generally outperforms the Stack and LinkedList classes for the same purpose. ArrayDeque is not thread-safe, but ConcurrentLinkedDeque is a thread-safe alternative.

Binary Search Tree

A binary search tree (BST) is a data structure that sorts nodes in a hierarchical tree. A red-black tree is a BST implementation that colors each node according to its location. The color of adjacent nodes can determine whether or not a tree is balanced. An unbalanced tree

non balanced

degrades to `O(n)` time on lookups, so a balancing operation is used after inserting or removing nodes to guarantee lookups in `O(log n)` time.

`TreeMap` is a red-black tree implementation that uses entry nodes to store its values. An `Entry` object contains a key, a value, a color, and a reference to its parent entry, left entry, and right entry. A `TreeMap` stores its entries according to the natural ordering of their keys or by a sorting strategy provided by a `Comparator`. A naturally sorted tree requires that keys correctly implement the `compareTo()` and `equals()` methods in the `Comparable` interface. A `TreeMap` iterates through its entries in sorted order. `TreeMap` is not thread-safe, but it can be decorated by the `Collections#synchronizedSortedMap()` method.

Heap

max heap
min heap

A heap is an unsorted data structure that organizes nodes in a hierarchical tree. In a *max-heap*, the values of a parent node are always greater than the values of its child nodes. In a *min-heap*, the values of a parent node are always less than the values of its child nodes.

A heap is a maximally efficient implementation of a priority queue. A priority queue serves elements according to their priority and falls back to a FIFO policy for identical priorities. The `PriorityQueue` class uses an object array to store its values. Although heaps are visually represented as a tree, they can be compactly stored inside of an array and nodes can be located by index arithmetic. `PriorityQueue` is not thread-safe, but `PriorityBlockingQueue` is a thread-safe alternative.

Set

A `Set` is a data structure that holds a collection of unique values. Sets often delegate functionality to maps because the keys in a map are already unique. `HashSet` utilizes a `HashMap`, which does not maintain the insertion order of its elements. `LinkedHashSet`

((

utilizes a `LinkedHashMap`, which maintains insertion order by way of an auxiliary `LinkedList`. `TreeSet` utilizes a `TreeMap`, which maintains the natural ordering of its elements. None of these classes are thread-safe, but the `Collections#newSetFromMap()` method can create a set out of a `ConcurrentHashMap`.

Iterator

An `Iterator` is an object that can visit and remove elements in a collection. A *fail-fast* iterator throws a `ConcurrentModificationException` if it detects structural changes to a collection outside of its `remove()` method. A *fail-safe* iterator will not throw an exception because it operates on a clone of the original collection.

Questions

What is the difference between an ArrayList and a LinkedList?

How does a HashMap work internally?

What would happen if a key's hashCode() or equals() method was incorrect?

What is the difference between a stack and a queue?

What is the difference between a binary search tree, red-black tree, and a heap?

What is the difference between a HashSet, LinkedHashSet, and TreeSet?

What is the difference between a fail-fast iterator
and a fail-safe iterator?

Important Interfaces

Autocloseable

The `Autocloseable` interface is used in a *try-with-resources* block
to cleanup resources. `Autocloseable` defines a `close()` method
that is invoked by the JVM after a *try-with-resources* block completes.

Comparable

The `Comparable` interface determines the natural ordering
between objects of the same type. `Comparable` defines a generic
`compareTo(T)` method that returns an integer indicating whether
an object is less than, equal to, or greater than a comparable object.
A list of `Comparable` objects can be sorted in the
`Collections#sort(List)` method.

Comparator

The `Comparator` interface determines a sorting strategy between objects
of the same type. This can be used to sort objects that do not implement
`Comparable`, or to sort objects in a manner distinct from their natural
ordering. `Comparator` defines a generic `compare(T, T)` method that
returns an integer indicating whether the first object is less than, equal to,
or greater than the second object. Lists can be sorted by comparators
in the `Collections#sort(List, Comparator)` method.

Iterable

The `Iterable` interface defines a method that returns an `Iterator`.
An object that implements `Iterable` can be used in an enhanced
for-loop. Note that although arrays can be used in enhanced for-loops,
they do not implement the `Iterable` interface.

Runnable

The Runnable interface encapsulates an action that runs inside of a thread. Runnable defines a run() method that is invoked by the thread scheduler after a thread transitions into a runnable state.

Callable

→ call method
→ used through executor framework

The Callable interface encapsulates a task that runs inside of a thread and computes a result. Callable defines a generic call() method that returns a result or throws an exception. Callable is used throughout the executor framework.

Serializable

The Serializable interface is a marker which indicates that an object is eligible for serialization. Serialization is the process of converting an object into bytes that can be stored on a filesystem or streamed over a network. Objects can provide custom serialization logic by implementing three special private methods: writeObject(), readObject(), and readObjectNoData(). Every serializable class is assigned a configurable version number called *serialVersionUID* that is used to ensure compatibility during the deserialization process.

Questions

What is the Autocloseable interface?

What is the Comparable interface?

What is the Comparator interface?

What is the Iterable interface?

What is the Runnable interface?

What is the Callable interface?

What is the Serializable interface?

Creational Design Patterns

Creational design patterns solve common problems that arise during the creation of objects.

Builder Pattern

The builder pattern provides an alternative to a constructor with an excessive number of parameters. A builder object temporarily stores the state of a new object through a chain of fluent method calls, until the target object is constructed in one final step. The `MapMaker` class in the Google Guava library is an example of the builder pattern.

Factory Pattern

The factory pattern provides an instance of an abstract class or an interface without burdening the client with implementation details. This is useful for encapsulating complicated creational logic or utilizing object pools for performance. The `Calendar#getInstance()` method is an example of the factory pattern.

Abstract Factory Pattern

The abstract factory pattern, also known as a factory of factories, provides instances of factory classes without burdening the client with implementation details. This is useful for encapsulating the creational logic of a set of related factory classes. The `DocumentBuilderFactory` class is an example of the abstract factory pattern.

Prototype Pattern

The prototype pattern creates a cloned object out of a prototype. This is useful when an object is prohibitively expensive to create, such as the result of a database query. The `Object#clone()` method is an example of the prototype pattern.

Singleton Pattern

The singleton pattern restricts the instantiation of a class to a single instance. Singletons are preferable to global variables because they can be lazily initialized, although some implementations require explicit synchronization to do so. The `Runtime#getInstance()` method is an example of the singleton pattern.

Questions

What is the builder pattern? When is it useful?

What is the factory pattern? When is it useful?

What is the abstract factory pattern? When is it useful?

What is the prototype pattern? When is it useful?

What is the singleton pattern? When is it useful?

Structural Design Patterns

Structural design patterns solve common problems that arise
due to the relationship between different objects.

Adapter Pattern

The adapter pattern converts an incompatible object into a form that
a module accepts. This allows separate modules of code to communicate
without coupling them together. The `Arrays#asList(Object[])`
method is an example of the adapter pattern.

Composite Pattern

The composite pattern treats a collection of objects as if it were
a single object. This is useful when a group of objects share similar
functionality, such as the elements of a Swing application.
The `Container#add(Component)` method is an example
of the composite pattern.

Decorator Pattern

The decorator pattern provides additional behavior to an object by
wrapping it with a delegator. This provides a flexible alternative to creating
multiple subclasses. The `Collections#unmodifiableList(List)`
method is an example of the decorator pattern.

Facade Pattern

The facade pattern provides a simplified interface over a large body of code.
This is useful when a system is complex or poorly designed and clients are
only interested in a subset of functionality. The `Logger` interface in the
SLF4J library is an example of the facade pattern.

Flyweight Pattern

The flyweight pattern reduces the memory footprint of an application by reusing objects. This is useful when a large number of immutable objects are frequently instantiated. The `Integer#valueOf(String)` method is an example of the flyweight pattern.

Questions

What is the adapter pattern? When is it useful?

What is the composite pattern? When is it useful?

What is the decorator pattern? When is it useful?

What is the facade pattern? When is it useful?

What is the flyweight pattern? When is it useful?

Behavioral Design Patterns

Behavioral design patterns solve common problems that arise due to the interaction of different objects.

Command Pattern

The command pattern encapsulates all of the information needed to execute an action. This is useful for operations that need to be invoked outside of the context in which they were created. The `Runnable` interface is an example of the command pattern.

Observer Pattern

The observer pattern notifies a collection of observers about state changes to a subject of interest. This is useful for decoupling a subject from the concerns of its followers. The `Observer` class and `Observable` interface are examples of the observer pattern.

Strategy Pattern

The strategy pattern dynamically chooses the behavior of an algorithm at runtime. This is useful for operations that have a variety of custom implementations. The `Collections#sort(List, Comparator)` method is an example of the strategy pattern.

Visitor Pattern

The visitor pattern separates an algorithm from the object structure on which it operates. This is useful when different algorithms need to traverse a similar path through a complex object. The `ElementVisitor` interface is an example of the visitor pattern.

Null Object Pattern

The null object pattern represents an object with neutral or empty behavior. This is useful to prevent excessive `null` checks in an application. The `Collections#emptyList()` method is an example of the null object pattern.

Questions

What is the command pattern? When is it useful?

What is the observer pattern? When is it useful?

What is the strategy pattern? When is it useful?

What is the visitor pattern? When is it useful?

What is the null object pattern? When is it useful?

Reflection

Reflection allows a program to manipulate an object at runtime without knowing about the object at compile time. For example, if you wanted to debug an object that didn't override the toString() method, you could use reflection to inspect every field. Reflection is possible due to a collection of classes that represent programming constructs such as Class, Field, and Method.

Class

A Class is a special object constructed by the JVM that represents classes and interfaces in an application. If you consider a class file as the blueprint for an object, you can consider the Class class as a blueprint for blueprints. A Class instance can be retrieved from an object by calling the getClass() method, or it can be looked up by its fully qualified name with the Class#forName() method.

A Class provides type introspection for an object. Type introspection allows a program to examine the properties of an object at runtime. For example, a Class object contains introspective methods such as getName(), getPackage(), getDeclaredFields(), and getDeclaredMethods(). A Class can also create an object with the newInstance() method. This is widely used in frameworks that need to instantiate objects defined in XML files.

Field

A Field provides access to a single field in a class or an interface. A Field contains introspective methods that allow you to get a value from a field, as well as reflective methods that allow you to a set a value into a field. However, a flag must be set on the Field object via

((

the setAccessible() method to allow access to fields
with limited visibility.

Method

A Method object provides access to a single method in a class
or interface. A Method contains introspective methods that provide
information about the method declaration, as well as reflective methods
that allow you to invoke the method. However, a flag must be set on the
Method object via the setAccessible() method to allow access
to methods with limited visibility.

Pros and Cons

Reflection is a powerful tool that plays a crucial role in countless extensions
to the Java library, such as test frameworks, IoC containers, ORM mappers,
profilers, and debuggers. On the other hand, Java is a strongly-typed
language that provides robust compile-time checking, and much of that
protection is lost with reflection. Reflection also breaks encapsulation
by allowing access to fields and methods outside of their intended scope.
Finally, reflection has slower performance than non-reflective code
due to the additional overhead on the JVM.

Questions

What is reflection?

What is type introspection?

What is a Class object?

What is a Field object?

What is a Method object?

What are some of the pros and cons of reflection?

Dependency Injection

Inversion of Control

Inversion of Control (IoC) is a pattern that decouples software components from their dependencies. For example, a password recovery service would need access to a service that could deliver emails. A password service with control over its dependencies would need to instantiate and configure an email service directly. A password service with inverted control over its dependencies would have an email service provided by some other object. A service that relinquishes control of its dependencies is more flexible because different implementations can be provided without changing any code in the service. For example, a mock email service could be injected during testing to avoid sending emails or to simulate a failure.

Service Locator vs Dependency Injection = IoC

Two common implementations of IoC are the service locator pattern and dependency injection. A service locator provides a central repository for objects to request dependencies. Dependency injection takes the inversion principle even further by allowing a container to inject dependencies directly into components through constructor arguments or setter methods.

Constructor Injection vs Setter Injection

Constructor injection requires a component to declare a constructor with arguments for every dependency. This allows any initialization logic to run in the constructor, but components with multiple dependencies may have unwieldy constructor declarations. Setter injection requires a component to declare setter methods for every dependency. Setter injection is more flexible, but any initialization logic must take place after all the

dependencies have been injected. In either case, a container is required
to manage the relationship between components and their dependencies.

The Spring Container

The Spring framework is one of the most popular extensions to the Java
language. Although the Spring library has spread into numerous domains,
the heart of the library is a dependency injection container. The Spring
container is responsible for instantiating, configuring, and injecting
components (called beans) into a running application.

Spring Configuration

The Spring container requires configuration that defines beans and their
relationship within an application. Configuration can be provided in the
form of XML, annotations, or java code. XML configuration is commonly
used due to its intuitive nature, but it's susceptible to refactoring errors
because the names of classes and packages often change. Annotations
provide an alternative to XML, but the resulting configuration is
decentralized and any changes require modifications to the source code.
Java configuration files combine the centralized configuration of XML
with the convenience of annotations, but it lacks some of the flexibility
that XML provides.

Spring Lifecycle

The Spring container begins by instantiating an `ApplicationContext`
with one of the available configuration options. The container instantiates
all of the beans and injects their dependencies via constructor injection,
setter injection, or reflection. Finally, the container invokes callback
methods on beans that hook into the lifecycle of the container.
For example, the container will invoke the `afterPropertiesSet()`
method on any bean that implements the `InitializingBean`
interface.

Questions

What is the inversion of control pattern?

What is the difference between a service locator
and dependency injection?

What is the difference between constructor injection
and setter injection?

What is the Spring container?

What are the different ways of configuring a Spring container?

What is the lifecycle of a Spring container?

Aspect-Oriented Programming

Core Concerns vs Cross-Cutting Concerns

A core concern is a unit of work that contributes to the business logic of an application, such as storing records in a database or generating reports. A cross-cutting concern is a feature that spans across core concerns and supports an application, such as logging or caching.

Aspect-Oriented Programming

Aspect-oriented programming (AOP) isolates cross-cutting concerns through the use of aspects. Aspects work by targeting a method, called a join point, and surrounding it with additional code. Join points are determined by an expression called a pointcut. For example, in order to find the slowest method in an application, you could declare a pointcut that targets all public methods and compare the time before and after each join point executes.

Proxy Objects

A simple way to implement aspect-oriented programming is through the use of proxy objects. A proxy is a wrapper that provides additional functionality to an object of interest. Proxies can be implemented through interfaces or inheritance.

Interface Proxies

An object that implements an interface can be proxied by another class that implements the same interface. For example, in order to log every method call on an `ArrayList`, you could create a `ProxyList` class that implements `List` and delegates every method to a private `ArrayList`.

Each delegated method provides a join point that can be surrounded by logging code.

This proxy could be passed to any method that accepts a `List`. However, one limitation of interface proxies is that any self-invoked method inside the composed object will not be proxied. For example, if the `remove()` method in `ArrayList` internally calls the `get()` method, that call will not be logged because the join point will never be invoked.

Inheritance Proxies

An object that is non-final can be proxied by another class that extends it. For example, in order to log every method call on an `ArrayList`, you could create a `ProxyList` class that extends `ArrayList` and overrides every method with a delegated call to `super()`. Each overridden method provides a join point that can be surrounded by logging code.

This proxy could be passed to any method that accepts a `List` or an `ArrayList`. However, one limitation of inheritance proxies is that final classes and final methods cannot be proxied.

Runtime Weaving vs Binary Weaving

Weaving is the process of linking aspects and objects together. Proxy objects are examples of runtime weaving, which can be accomplished through pure coding patterns. Binary weaving injects aspects directly into bytecode. Binary weaving can take place at compile-time with a custom compiler or at load-time with a custom class loader. Binary weaving has none of the limitations of interface or inheritance proxies, but it usually requires the help of a dedicated library.

AspectJ

AspectJ is a widely used AOP framework with support for compile-time weaving, load-time weaving, and post-compile weaving for external classes. AspectJ is often used in conjunction with the Spring framework, which provides additional support for aspects as well as runtime weaving.

Questions

What is the difference between a core concern and a cross-cutting concern?

What is aspect-oriented programming?

What is the difference between an interface proxy and an inheritance proxy?

What is the difference between runtime weaving and binary weaving?

What is the AspectJ library?

Unit Testing

Test-Driven Development

Test-driven development (TDD) encourages loosely coupled, highly cohesive, and frequently tested modules of code. The TDD cycle begins by writing an automated test case for functionality that doesn't exist. Then, a developer produces the minimum amount of code needed to make the test succeed. As more and more test cases are added, a comprehensive test suite emerges that can detect and prevent bugs caused by new functionality.

TDD can also be applied to bug fixing. Writing a test case before fixing a bug will determine whether a fix was effective and at the same time guarantee that the bug will never resurface.

Unit Tests

A unit test relies on assertions to verify the behavior of code. An assertion throws an error if an expectation isn't met, such as when a field doesn't match an expected value. A unit test succeeds if it completes without falling any assertions or throwing any exceptions. Java provides the `assert` keyword, but it relies on JVM arguments to enable and it's preferable to use a framework with more flexibility. JUnit is a popular unit testing framework that includes a rich API for assertions as well as support for test fixtures.

Test Fixtures

A test fixture is a fixed state of objects used as a baseline for running tests. For example, a test fixture could drop and recreate an in-memory database to allow data access tests to work on a clean set of data after every test execution.

Mock Objects

Mock objects mimic the behavior of objects that are too impractical to incorporate into unit tests. For example, it would be prohibitive to charge a credit card or launch a missile every time a unit test runs. Mock objects implement the same interface as the objects they mimic, allowing developers to simulate controlled scenarios without modifying the code that's being tested. Mock objects can be created manually, but frameworks such as Mockito provide powerful proxies that can trace and verify the behavior of method calls.

Questions

What is test-driven development? Why is it beneficial?

What is a unit test?

What is JUnit?

What are text fixtures?

What are mock objects?

Programming Problems

How to Approach Programming Problems

During the interview you may be asked to solve high-level programming problems. In order to demonstrate a healthy approach to problem solving, follow these steps:

1) Restate the problem to ensure that you understand it correctly.

2) Provide a simple solution regardless of efficiency.

3) Critique your solution and analyze it for optimizations.

Identifying the nature of a problem can help you solve it. For example, problems that require repetitive steps lend themselves well to recursion. Problems involving collections of data often utilize existing data structures. Practice solving sample problems and study the process of discovering a solution rather than memorizing the solution itself.

Sample Programming Problems

How would you write a method that calculates the factorial of a number?

A factorial is the product of an integer and all of the integers below it (4! = 4*3*2*1). A factorial is a naturally recursive operation, which is apparent if you visualize the formula as part of the solution (4 * 3!). The formula can then be converted into a recursive method call: n * factorial(n - 1). However, the first line in a recursive algorithm should define a termination condition. Here, an input of 1 requires no recursion because the result is simply 1.

Recursive methods are slower than loops due to the overhead of method invocations. A recursive method can be converted to an iterative method by creating a loop that steps towards the termination condition and updates the state of local variables. In practice, you should always favor simplicity over premature optimization, but in the context of an interview you should be as critical as possible.

How would you determine whether a string is a palindrome?

A palindrome is a word that is identical forwards and backwards. A simple solution is to reverse the string and compare it to the original. There is no reverse method in the `String` class, but you could use the `StringBuilder#reverse()` method or a recursive formula: `hello = o + reverse(hell)`.

Rather than create additional `String` instances, a more efficient solution would use the `String#charAt()` method with pointers on both ends converging towards the middle of the string. If each character matches before the pointers converge, the string is a palindrome.

Given a line of text, how would you verify that the number of open and closed parentheses are balanced?

In order to simplify this problem, you could ignore the irrelevant characters and add all of the parentheses to a string. Then, you could recursively loop through the string and remove every immediate pair of open and closed parentheses `(()())` -> `()`. When the string has no more pairs, the number of remaining characters will determine if the parentheses were balanced.

As an optimization, every time you add a closed parenthesis to the string you could check to see if the last character was an open parenthesis and discard them both instead. In fact, there would be no need for recursion if you did this because you are essentially treating the string like a stack. Knowing that, you could solve this problem efficiently by using

use stack push open paranthesis a value when you see opening paranthesis pop a value when when u see closing paranthesis
for closing

an `ArrayDeque` to push and pop open parentheses and checking if the stack was empty afterwards.

Given an unsorted list with one missing number from 1 to 100, how would you determine the missing number?

The simplest solution to this problem is to iterate through the list 100 times and search for a specific value during each iteration. However, it's worth criticizing any solution that runs in quadratic time. If you sort the list first, you could find the number that didn't correspond to an appropriate index in linearithmic time. Faster still, you could put each value into a `HashSet`, and find the missing value in linear time.

It's impossible to solve this problem faster than linear time, but it's important to note that time complexity only measures the growth rate of an algorithm. In fact, this problem can be solved more efficiently by computing the sum of all numbers and subtracting it from the total sum provided by the formula `n(n+1)/2`. Whenever you critique a solution, remember to take memory into consideration when time complexity is no longer a factor.

Interview Preparation

Before the Interview

The best way to prepare for an interview is to study. You only have a short time to convince someone that you're worth hiring, so you want to appear knowledgeable and confident. Keep in mind that some topics may be outside the scope of this guide, such as relational databases, front end web development, or algorithm design. Try not to get overwhelmed by the amount of information out there. The majority of interviewers believe that a candidate with strong fundamentals is capable of learning new technologies quickly.

Before your interview, get a good night's sleep, eat a healthy breakfast, and wear a suit to look your best. Confirm your appointment and plan to arrive at least a half hour early. If you are doing a phone interview, charge your phone, bring a bottle of water, and find a quiet place where you won't get distracted.

During the Interview

A technical interview usually begins with casual questions about your background, such as:

Could you tell us about yourself and your experience?

Could you tell us about any side projects you've worked on?

Could you tell us about a time you solved a particularly challenging problem?

Could you tell us about a time you resolved a disagreement with a coworker?

What was your previous development environment like?

Why you are interested in working at our company?

Why you are leaving your previous job?

What is your biggest weakness? What is your biggest strength?

During the technical interview, do your best to answer the interviewer's questions in your own words. If you are unfamiliar with a topic, it's much better to admit that rather than bullshit your way through it. If you are on the phone, don't try to look up an answer on google. It's exceedingly obvious when a candidate stalls, taps away on their keyboard, and spits out a flawless response thirty seconds later.

During the wrap up, you will usually be asked if you have any questions. You should always ask at least one, but never ask about salary or benefits. You are trying to advertise what you can do for a company, not what a company can do for you. Some examples questions are:

What is the culture like at your company?

What is the development environment like at your company?

What is the software development lifecycle at your company?

Is there anything about me that you are concerned about?

Is there anything I should learn while waiting for your response?

What was the correct answer to <a question that you missed>?

What are the next steps?

After the Interview

Every interview is a learning experience. Regardless of whether or not you get the job, you'll gain valuable knowledge about the interview process. Write down all of the questions you were asked and research the ones that were difficult for you. They will be a valuable resource in the future, especially when you are the one conducting the interviews!

Have fun, and good luck!

Interview Questions

The Java Programming Language

What is the WORA principle? Why is it beneficial?

How can Java applications run on multiple platforms?

What is the difference between the JRE and the JDK?

What is the difference between procedural programming and object-oriented programming?

Object-Oriented Concepts

What is the purpose of abstraction in software development?

What is encapsulation? How does Java support it?

What is polymorphism? How does Java support it?

What is the difference between a mutable object and an immutable object?

How can you design an object to be immutable?

What is the difference between coupling and cohesion?

What is the preferred relationship between software components and why?

Object-Oriented Programming (Part I)

What is the difference between a class and an object?

What happens when an object is instantiated for the first time?

What is the difference between a primitive type and an object?

What is the difference between autoboxing and unboxing?

What is an array?

How is a String different from a regular object?

What is the difference between a StringBuilder and a StringBuffer?

Why are enums superior to String or Integer constants?

What is the difference between package-by-layer
and package-by-feature?

Object-Oriented Programming (Part II)

What is the difference between a method declaration
and a method signature?

What is a recursive method?

What is the final keyword used for?

What is the static keyword used for?

Why can't a static method access a nonstatic field?

What are access modifiers used for? What are the different types?

What are annotations used for?

The Object Superclass

What is the difference between a shallow copy and a deep copy?

Why is a copy constructor preferable to the clone method?

What is the difference between the identity operator
and the equals() method?

What is the relationship between the hashCode() method
and the equals() method?

What is the default implementation of the toString() method?

Why is the finalize() method unreliable for cleanup operations?

Composition & Inheritance

What is the difference between composition and inheritance?

What is the difference between method overriding
and method overloading?

How would you determine whether to use composition
or inheritance?

((

Abstract Classes & Interfaces

What is the difference between an abstract class and an interface?

How would you determine whether to use an abstract class or an interface?

Why can't a class be declared both final and abstract?

What is the value of designing a codebase around the use of interfaces?

What are anonymous classes used for?

What is a closure?

What is a lambda expression?

Exceptions

What is an exception?

What is the difference between an unchecked and a checked exception?

How would you determine whether to use an unchecked or a checked exception?

How does a try/catch/finally block work?

How does the try-with-resources statement work?

Generics

What is the difference between a compile-time error and a runtime error?

What is the purpose of generics?

What are the different types of generic wildcards?

What is type erasure?

What are some of the limitations of generics?

Concurrency

What is the lifecycle of a Thread?

Why is synchronization necessary on shared resources?

What is used as a lock for synchronized static and synchronized non-static methods?

What would happen if two different threads hit two synchronized non-static methods on the same object simultaneously?

What would happen if two different threads hit a synchronized static method and synchronized non-static method on the same object simultaneously?

What one thing does the volatile keyword guarantee about a variable?

What two things does the synchronize keyword guarantee about a block of code?

What are some built-in concurrent data structures?

What is the executor framework?

What is a ThreadLocal variable?

What are atomic variables?

Memory Management

How does the JVM divide memory on the heap?

What is the standard algorithm for garbage collection?

What are memory leaks? How can they be identified?

What are the four different types of references?

What is a ReferenceQueue?

Why is a phantom reference safer than using the finalize() method?

Java Database Connectivity

What is JDBC?

What are the two ways of acquiring a Connection object?

What is the difference between the three types of Statements?

What is a ResultSet?

What is an SQL injection attack? How can it be prevented?

What are the advantages and disadvantages
of object-relational mapping?

What is Hibernate?

Web Applications

What is a servlet container?

What is a web application?

What is a WAR file?

What is a web.xml file?

What is the difference between a Servlet and an HttpServlet?

What is the difference between a Servlet and a JSP?

What is a servlet filter?

What is the model-view-controller pattern?

Web Services

What is service-oriented architecture?

What are web services?

What is the difference between a SOAP web service
and a REST web service?

What is the difference between JAX-WS and JAX-RS?

What are some frameworks that aid in the development
of Java web services?

Algorithms

What is Big O notation? What are some common examples?

What is a binary search? How well does it perform?

What is insertion sort? How well does it perform?

What is merge sort? How well does it perform?

What is quicksort? How well does it perform?

What is timsort? How well does it perform?

Java Collections Framework

What is the difference between an ArrayList and a LinkedList?

How does a HashMap work internally?

What would happen if a key's hashCode() or equals() method was incorrect?

What is the difference between a stack and a queue?

What is the difference between a binary search tree, red-black tree, and a heap?

What is the difference between a HashSet, LinkedHashSet, and TreeSet?

What is the difference between a fail-fast iterator and a fail-safe iterator?

Important Interfaces

What is the Autocloseable interface?

What is the Comparable interface?

What is the Comparator interface?

What is the Iterable interface?

What is the Runnable interface?

What is the Callable interface?

What is the Serializable interface?

Creational Design Patterns

What is the builder pattern? When is it useful?

What is the factory pattern? When is it useful?

What is the abstract factory pattern? When is it useful?

What is the prototype pattern? When is it useful?

What is the singleton pattern? When is it useful?

Structural Design Patterns

What is the adapter pattern? When is it useful?

What is the composite pattern? When is it useful?

What is the decorator pattern? When is it useful?

What is the facade pattern? When is it useful?

What is the flyweight pattern? When is it useful?

Behavioral Design Patterns

What is the command pattern? When is it useful?

What is the observer pattern? When is it useful?

What is the strategy pattern? When is it useful?

What is the visitor pattern? When is it useful?

What is the null object pattern? When is it useful?

Reflection

What is reflection?

What is type introspection?

What is a Class object?

What is a Field object?

What is a Method object?

What are some of the pros and cons of reflection?

Dependency Injection

What is the inversion of control pattern?

What is the difference between a service locator
and dependency injection?

What is the difference between constructor injection
and setter injection?

What is the Spring container?

What are the different ways of configuring a Spring container?

What is the lifecycle of a Spring container?

Aspect-Oriented Programming

What is the difference between a core concern
and a cross-cutting concern?

What is aspect-oriented programming?

What is the difference between an interface proxy
and an inheritance proxy?

What is the difference between runtime weaving
and binary weaving?

What is the AspectJ library?

Unit Testing

What is test-driven development? Why is it beneficial?

What is a unit test?

What is JUnit?

What are text fixtures?

What are mock objects?

Programming Problems

How would you write a method that calculates the factorial of a number?

How would you determine whether a string is a palindrome?

Given a line of text, how would you verify that the number of open and closed parentheses are balanced?

Given an unsorted list with one missing number from 1 to 100, how would you determine the missing number?

Personal Questions

Could you tell us about yourself and your experience?

Could you tell us about any side projects you've worked on?

Could you tell us about a time you solved a particularly challenging problem?

Could you tell us about a time you resolved a disagreement
with a coworker?

What was your previous development environment like?

Why you are interested in working at our company?

Why you are leaving your previous job?

What is your biggest weakness? What is your biggest strength?

About the Author

Anthony DePalma is a Java aficionado who's conducted over 100 interviews at Fortune 500 companies. When he's not programming he can be found surfing the beautiful hurricanes of New Jersey. He lives down the shore with his wife and two cats. Java Interview Guide is his first book.

For more information please visit
www.javainterviewguide.com

Notes

Notes

Made in the USA
San Bernardino, CA
13 January 2017